Against All Odds:

Success After Teen Pregnancy

Against All Odds:
Success After Teen Pregnancy
by
Cynthia A. Cass

Fulton Press

Dallas, Texas

Against All Odds: Success After Teen Pregnancy

For the sake of their privacy, some people in my story will not be identified by their true names.

Published by Fulton Press, P.O. Box 151634, Dallas, TX 75315.

Edited by Frances Whiteside

Cover Photograph by: Glamour Shots

Library of Congress Catalog Card Number: 98-93652

ISBN: 1-57502-961-8

Printed in the USA by

MORRIS PUBLISHING

3212 East Highway 30   Kearney, NE 68847   1-800-650-7888

Dedication

To Tameka, my daughter and the love of my life:

You were the driving force and motivation in my struggle to achieve success and independence in spite of the odds. We made it!

To Teenage and Single Mothers:

This book is also dedicated to you. Self-sufficiency is possible with hard work, determination and the ability to believe in yourself. Make parenting your children the No. 1 priority in your life. In order to succeed, you must think positive about the future. You <u>can</u> overcome any obstacles. Continue your education. It's the key to attaining your goals. Remember, the choices you make as a parent will affect your children for a lifetime.

Acknowledgments

Special Thanks to:

- Lorenzo Horton - for putting an end to the abuse

- Mary Mingo - for believing in me

- Audrey Meer - for teaching me the value of a good attitude

- Gwendolyn Davis, Tameka's fifth grade English teacher - for your love and discipline

- Anne Schuler - for introducing me to the concept of excellence

- Robert Parish - for your support and encouragement

- Mary McLennan, Gloria Hill, Christa Mangrum, Demetria Carter, and DeDe Meyers - for your enthusiastic critiquing

- Frances Whiteside, my editor

- Tameka - for nagging me until I finished the book

- My Pastor - for your inspiring message from the pulpit that impressed upon me the need to complete my manuscript

CONTENTS

Introduction

I decided to write this book to share my personal experiences as a teenage, single parent. Although my journey was not easy, the prize of self-sufficiency made the struggle worthwhile.

Initially, the odds seemed insurmountable because I had so much to overcome.

I'd never met my birth mother.

I was raised in an abusive home.

I was pregnant at 15.

I became a mother at 16.

My father died when I was 17.

I was forced to move from home during my senior year of high school with a year-old baby.

But I refused to allow those circumstances to determine my place in life. My goal was to be a good parent and role model for my daughter. I was determined to obtain a college degree, establish a career and avoid all the stereotypes that are associated with unwed teen mothers.

Over the years, I've read the statistics. Society expected me to fail once I became pregnant at the age of 15. According to the statistics:

- If you have a child out of wedlock, more will follow.

- You will probably become dependent on government assistance (e.g., welfare, food stamps, public housing).

- You are not likely to finish high school or attend college.

- History will repeat itself with your children and the next generation.

- Your lack of maturity and parenting skills will produce troubled, unstable children.

- Your future employment opportunities will be limited to low-wage jobs.

- You will live a life of poverty.

The statistics were too depressing for me to accept. Instead I decided to overcome the odds and become self-reliant. In order to achieve my goal, I took specific steps to ensure my success. First, I finished high school. Next, after working at numerous low-wage jobs, I continued my education. Finally, I chose not to have any more children out of wedlock.

This book is not a day-by-day autobiography. Instead, it is a selection of remembrances, situations, and periods in my life -- whether joyous or painful -- that shaped my moral character and made me the person I am today. Along the way I encountered pitfalls to be avoided: becoming involved in abusive relationships and steering clear of drug and alcohol abuse. I focused on goals that would ensure my success:

maintaining stable employment and making parenting my first priority.

A friend who critiqued my book asked, "What if a young girl that wants to have a baby uses your book as justification that she can have a baby and succeed?" My answer: If you're a young girl who is lonely, having a baby won't change that. Motherhood is a demanding, full-time job. You will be overwhelmed with responsibilities.

This book was not written to encourage teen pregnancy. It was written to focus on ways to achieve success after becoming a teen parent. My purpose in writing this book was to show that by not repeating that same mistake over and over again, success is possible. If you continue to have more children while unmarried, you reduce your chances to become self-reliant.

I started writing this book six years ago. I would write for a while and put it down. I kept telling myself that I was just a regular person, and regular people don't write books. But each time I put the project aside, I would meet a young woman in a situation similar to the one I had survived. Sometimes a friend or neighbor would tell me a story of a teenage or single mother who could, I believed, be encouraged by reading my story. I met an attorney who recalled a case where he was court-appointed to represent a 14-year-old African-American girl who was charged with minor shoplifting. He arranged probation in the case and took her to lunch after court. He asked about her plans for the future. She replied, "Now that I have my period, I guess that in a year or so I'll begin to have children so I can get my welfare and food stamps started like my older sister." He was shocked at the sincerity and determination in her voice.

When you are born into a certain environment or have despairing circumstances develop, you must be offered hope and shown role models to realize you can succeed.

Developing the manuscript was therapy in itself from a personal standpoint. I'd write a chapter and wonder, "How did I ever get through that?" Retelling certain parts of my early life history has been very painful, offering me another excuse to stop writing.

My book offers hope to both teenage and single mothers, because often they are one and the same. Teen pregnancy and single parenting crosses all racial, ethnic, and economic lines.

Over and over I'm asked, "Why didn't you give up? How did you have the determination to go on despite all the obstacles?" The answer is twofold: I have a strong faith and belief in God, and I was determined to survive. I had a responsibility and commitment to provide Tammy with a better life than mine.

Today, both Tammy and I have accomplished personal goals that seemed unreachable when I look back on the obstacles we had to overcome.

In 1988, I started college at age 32. Working full-time, I took four years to complete a two-year program. Two months after I graduated, I started school again, continued for an additional two years and in 1994, at the age of 38, earned a bachelor of science degree in business management.

Tammy has two associate degrees, one in social work and one in substance abuse. She is completing her bachelors degree while maintaining a full-time job.

We've come a long way from that one-room efficiency apartment I rented when I moved out on my own at age 17. I hope this book inspires other young mothers and single parents of all ages to strive for success and economic independence.

Chapter One

The Beginning

My childhood was one big mess. I don't remember my mother because she and my dad split when I was two years old. I was not told her side of the story. Daddy said it happened because he came home from work to pick up the lunch he'd forgotten and found her boyfriend visiting.

But, what goes around sure comes around. When my father Harry was a young man, he married a lady from Jefferson, Texas, named Bessie Lee. They moved to California and rented an apartment. A couple named Vivian and Pete lived in the same complex. My daddy and Vivian began an affair. They were all members of a big dance club. One Saturday night there was a problem with the sound system. My daddy left Bessie Lee at a table to go and fix the stereo problem, and that's the last time she laid eyes on him for 25 years. He and Vivian ran away that night.

Daddy and Vivian moved to Arizona where my oldest sister Linda was born. They stayed in Arizona for a year and returned to California. Shortly after, my sister Brenda and I were born a year apart.

My daddy told us that after he caught Vivian with her man, he and Vivian battled back and forth for custody of us. In those days, the mother usually won. Once Vivian won custody, Daddy left California. He returned to Denver to stay with his mother. Grandmother remembered Daddy would come back from work every night, sit on the porch and cry for us.

Soon, Vivian called because she didn't have a job and was unable to take care of us. She told Grandmother she didn't have food and asked Grandmother to take us for a few months until she could find a job. She had never worked. Grandmother agreed and rode the train to California to pick us up, promising to return us as soon as Vivian was stable. I was two years old.

That was the last time my mother saw us as children.

Twice in my early years, when I was five and again when I was nine, we were packed up with all of our clothes and toys. We stayed in the country with a nice white family many miles away. Daddy worked with the man. Each time our country visit lasted about ten days. When I was 18, my Grandmother told me on those two occasions my mother came to town looking for us. My daddy told Vivian he had put us up for adoption because he couldn't afford to care for us. Grandmother said Daddy and Vivian had a mutual friend in California who called both times to warn him Vivian was coming. I still don't know what to believe.

When I was five years old, Daddy married a lady named Dorothy. She was nice to me, but she drank too much. My dad didn't drink at all, so he broke up with Dorothy. It was hard for

Daddy to raise three girls alone. When I was six years old, Daddy had a TV repair service. He had to work, comb our hair, help with homework, and be sure we were clean and dressed properly for school. Our grandmother came by once or twice a week to check on us, especially if Daddy had to work late. During prosperous times, Daddy always drove a Cadillac. He loved his car, but I was ashamed to be seen in such a big, wide car. I'd always ask Daddy, "Why can't we have a small car like a Beetle Bug?" Daddy would always laugh and say, "One day you'll understand."

Daddy became ill and was unable to work for a long time. He was in bed for many weeks. I didn't know what was wrong with him. One day a man knocked at the door and asked to speak to Daddy. Daddy said a few words to the man, then went to the table and picked up his key ring. He returned to the door, removed a few keys from the ring and handed the key ring to the man. Another man who had been waiting outside got into our car and drove away. Daddy went into the bathroom and shut the door. I could hear loud sobs coming from the bathroom. When Daddy came out, I could tell he had been crying. That was the last time we saw our car. We still had the van Daddy used to do his TV repair work. I will never forget that night when Daddy cried about his car. He explained to us that the men came to get the car because his business was slow and he couldn't afford to pay for the car any more. I found out later Daddy was sick because he had diabetes.

The story keeps twisting and turning. Twenty-five years after Daddy left Bessie Lee, she came to Denver from Dallas for a visit. The next thing I knew, Daddy said he was going to remarry her and we'd all move to Dallas. Bessie Lee was a school teacher. He said she loved us and because we were getting to be big girls, we needed another mother. We were 11, 12, and 14. I was excited about having another mother, but I missed Dorothy.

My happiness was short-lived. On our second day in Dallas, Bessie Lee washed Brenda's mouth out with Ivory soap. It was the beginning of an extremely abusive relationship. Soon Bessie Lee was saying, "You're all tramps, just like your mother." I was afraid of her. While my father was at work, we'd get beatings for little or no reason. When he was at home, he chose to ignore our screams. Perhaps Daddy felt guilty because he'd left Bessie Lee for our mother 25 years earlier and, because of his guilt, he allowed Bessie Lee to abuse us. I've never understood.

Life with Bessie Lee was rough for a teenager. I was not allowed to participate in any extracurricular activities, except for the spelling bee, which I won in the seventh grade. We were not allowed to go to any school functions, parties, or events. I was not allowed to visit friends, and they couldn't visit me.

One of our biggest problems was the way Bessie Lee dressed us. Kids at school laughed at us because we dressed like old ladies. Soon we figured out how to get around Bessie Lee's dress code. Linda showed Brenda and me how to lift the lining of our winter coat to pin in an outfit that we had shortened or borrowed from a friend.

Makeup was also not allowed in our house. Once I got to school and put on the hidden outfit and enough makeup for two people, I felt just fine. False eyelashes were in style, and I took my lunch money and bought a pair for 99 cents. Once I forgot them, and when I came home from school they were swimming in the toilet. I bought a new pair the next morning.

The pinning method worked well in the winter, but when spring and summer came, we didn't have the coats to pin our clothes in. I began to sneak my outfit for the next day into the tool shed each night. Once Bessie Lee left for school, I'd make the corner and go into the shed and change my clothes. One evening, Bessie Lee went into the shed for a tool and found my outfit. She removed it without saying anything. The next morning after she left for school, I went to the shed in my old lady clothes and discovered my outfit was gone. I had to go to school in the old clothes. I was so embarrassed.

The verbal and physical abuse became the norm in our household until Mr. Horton came along. He was a counselor at our high school, a tall, handsome man in his forties. Our gym teacher, Ms. Cotton, reported Linda's bruises to him. He scheduled an appointment to visit our house and told Bessie Lee the beatings would have to stop. Bessie Lee began to beat us on Fridays so the bruises would be gone by Monday. We reported back to Mr. Horton. He came out again and told both Bessie Lee and Daddy if we got any more whippings he would see to it that we were removed from the home. The physical abuse stopped, but the verbal abuse escalated.

Chapter Two

Pregnant

I struggled to drink the mixture of hot sauce and vinegar. It was sure to make my period come. Soaking in hot water and Epsom salts sure hadn't worked.

Maybe my period was just late because I was so worried about it. Whatever the reason, I prayed day and night. It was already two weeks late, and I was beginning to wonder if maybe I could be pregnant. But that was impossible, because I'd only had sex one time -- and besides, Curtis Ray had told me he couldn't have children.

I was 15 years old and a sophomore at Lincoln High School in Dallas. My best friend Rita had the cutest brother named Curtis Ray. He was 23 years old and had just returned from the Army in a shiny new red Camaro. How I loved that

16

car! Curtis Ray was always flirting with me and asking if he could be my boyfriend. I was not allowed to "have company" until my sixteenth birthday, and that was almost a whole year away. Curtis Ray came over to meet my parents and ask if I could take company. He lied to my father about his age and, to impress my daddy, even said he was on the football team at school. But the answer was still no. I couldn't take company until next year.

One Saturday, I was walking to the grocery store when he passed and asked if I wanted a ride. I jumped at the chance to be with him and ride in the Camaro. He said he'd call me later in the week to come over to his house during the day because we needed to talk. I agreed. The date was set for Friday. He picked me up from school in front of all my friends. They made such a big deal about the car. We drove to his house. He said he would not force me to do anything I didn't want to do. Next, he gave me the longest, wettest kiss of my life. It wasn't sloppy, and he didn't cover and suck my whole mouth and nose like T.J. (the only other boy that ever kissed me). Curtis Ray and I had sex that day. Later in the afternoon he took me back to school.

I realize now I was too young and totally unprepared for sex. Sex was never discussed in our home. If two people started to kiss passionately on TV, my daddy would say, "It's time for bed." I always wondered what happened after those kisses. I found out the day I skipped school to "talk" to Curtis Ray.

Even my menstrual cycle was not explained by my stepmother. When I was 11½, I was sitting on our screened-in porch with my legs up. All of a sudden I felt like I was using the bathroom on myself. When I looked down and saw something red, I ran into the bathroom and locked the door, convinced I had cut myself. I called my sisters into the bathroom and told them I'd been cut. They laughed until they cried. I put them out of the bathroom and continued to look for the cut, but couldn't find it. Finally, Linda knocked on the door and told me I wasn't cut. She said, "You've started on your period." It scared me to death. She explained it to me and gave me a sanitary pad. I thought everybody at school would know I was on my period just by looking at me.

My coke-bottle shape was quickly changing. My belly was getting fat. I told my sister Linda I might be pregnant. She asked me some questions about what happened that day and decided to sneak me to the doctor for a pregnancy test. I was so scared. The test was positive. After having sex one time, I was pregnant.

Now I had to break the news to my father and stepmother. Linda said she'd come over on Thursday night to tell them for me. Thursday came quickly. We were all in the den watching the news. Linda said, "Daddy, Cynthia's pregnant." Time stood still -- it seemed like a long time before anybody said anything. My daddy hollered Linda's words back as though he had to say them to believe it. My stepmother started to curse. She called me terrible names. I was humiliated and scared to death.

Daddy demanded that Curtis Ray come over to talk. I called, and he came over with a sullen, angry look on his face. It was my first time seeing or talking to him since that day. I was hurt. Curtis Ray had lied when he said he couldn't have children. Daddy told him that we needed to get married to give the baby a name. He agreed, but looked like he had just been handed a death sentence. I couldn't believe this was the same guy who had told me he loved me. He didn't love me at all.

I made up my mind at that moment that I would not marry Curtis Ray. It was obvious that he had no feelings for me. I felt used. When he left, I told my Daddy that I wasn't going to marry Curtis Ray. Daddy became angry and argued with me for hours, but I stood my ground.

About six months later Daddy had his first stroke at the age of 55. He was unable to feed himself or walk without his cane. He was unable to return to work as an electrical engineer. Bessie Lee decided to resign her teaching position at the end of the year so we could move to a house they had recently built in Jefferson. Linda and Brenda refused to move. Linda married Albert, and Brenda moved to Denver to stay with my grandmother. As I packed for the move to Jefferson, I felt abandoned and alone.

Chapter Three

The Birth

After finding out in May I was pregnant, my parents were eager to move because they were so embarrassed. They kept my pregnancy a secret, especially at church. Once the move to Jefferson was completed in June 1971, culture shock occurred. We lived nine miles from town and the nearest hospital. It was hot and boring. Some people still had outside toilets. Our house was nice and new, but I was miserable. We were surrounded by elderly widow women. I didn't have a single friend or anybody my age to talk to. I almost ran away when I got my first prenatal exam. I wondered if I would die during the delivery. I was so naive that I questioned how a baby was going to come out of my stomach. I had so many questions but nobody to ask because Bessie Lee had never had a baby.

I checked the mail each day hoping to get a letter from Curtis Ray. After all, I was five months pregnant with his child. I never heard from him once after we moved. Not once. I wrote him letter after letter at the last address I had, but the letters were returned. He had moved without a forwarding address.

My due date was November 30th, but Tammy wouldn't wait. On October 9th, a sharp pain hit me in the middle of the night. I woke up Bessie Lee and Daddy and said I thought it was time. Bessie Lee told me to go back to bed. I tried but returned an hour later crying. At 5:00 a.m. we dressed and started the nine-mile drive to the hospital. For the next 12 hours I was in labor. It felt like a little alien was trying to fight its way out of my womb.

At 5:30 p.m. on October 10, 1972, Tameka Yhamon Cass entered the world. I had a beautiful baby girl with a coffee cream complexion and jet black hair that was long enough to go past the little bend in her neck. She had perfect almond-shaped eyes and a little pug nose. As soon as I saw her, she looked at me as if to say, "I need you." I took one look, and my heart flooded with love for her. I decided that instant to be the best mother I could be.

I just didn't know how hard it was going to be.

Chapter Four

Back to School

As soon as I got Tammy home, Bessie Lee took over. She was crazy about Tammy and took good care of her. I think Bessie Lee felt that Tammy was the baby she'd never had. I planned to enter Jefferson High after the Christmas break. Bessie Lee and Daddy agreed to keep the baby while I returned to finish the eleventh grade.

The day finally came for me to enroll at Jefferson High. I was nervous because I didn't know a soul. I was terrified to leave the office. When I was taken to my first class, all the guys were looking me over, and some of the girls were rolling their eyes. Some parents didn't want their kids to associate with me because I had a baby.

My stay at Jefferson High was bittersweet. I settled into the routine of school and began to make good grades. The Miss Jefferson High Contest was approaching, and one of my teachers nominated me to run. I was excited and began to make plans on what to wear in the contest. Everyone said I was sure to win.

The next day I was called into the school office by the assistant principal, a friend of Bessie Lee's, to discuss the contest. He began by saying how well the students liked me. He said I was pretty and admitted I had a good chance to win. But, he continued, he didn't think my running for the Miss Jefferson contest was a good idea, although he couldn't forbid me to enter. He explained that, because I had a baby and this was a small southern town, my running -- especially if I won -- would cause a major uproar. He warned I would probably be stripped of the title and written up in the school and city newspapers because I was not married and had a baby.

I immediately went to the nominating committee and withdrew, then I went home to cry. But once I held Tammy and she kissed me, I knew I'd made the right decision.

The rest of the year passed quickly. I made good grades and was looking forward to visiting Linda in Dallas for the summer. I wanted to take Tammy to see her daddy. I still checked the mailbox every day hoping to get a letter from Curtis Ray.

When Tammy was seven months old, we went to Dallas to spend the summer with Linda and her husband Albert. I ran into a friend of Curtis Ray's who gave me his address. The only contact I'd had with him in months was to call his sister Lois to tell her Tammy was born. Lois told Curtis Ray, and eventually he called me to ask who Tammy looked like. She was the spitting image of him.

I dressed Tammy up in a lacy pink dress with matching socks. I couldn't wait for her father to see her. I thought once he saw Tammy, he'd start to take care of her. Tammy's hair was perfect, and she smelled like fresh baby lotion. I walked up to the apartment door and knocked, expecting Curtis Ray to open the door and take us in his arms with hugs and kisses.

After I had knocked again, the door was opened by a large pregnant woman with her hair standing all over her head. I was shocked. I asked if Curtis Ray was there and she said, "No, but I'm his wife." I explained to her who I was and gave her my sister's number for Curtis Ray to call me. As soon as she shut the door, I began to cry. I cried all the way home.

Curtis Ray never called, but on the day we were to leave he came by to see Tammy. His reaction: "She's cute." He made no offer of diaper money, milk or anything else.

Summer had ended, and it was time to head back to Jefferson to begin my senior year of high school.

Chapter Five

On My Own

December 5, 1973. I was 17, sitting in my English class at Jefferson High School. An office aide asked to speak with me in the hall. She told me my father had just died. I was in shock -- not crying, just unable to believe my daddy had passed away. Daddy had suffered another stroke, but he died of emphysema after smoking since he was a teenager. I somehow made it through the funeral, but I felt as though my whole life was unraveling. I constantly wondered, "What's going to happen to Tammy and me?"

I was right to wonder. One month after my father died, after a particularly abusive insult from my stepmother, I decided it was time to move. She made it clear that it was impossible for Tammy and me to stay with her until I graduated. I remember crying at school because Bessie Lee said I had killed my daddy. It was a lie. My daddy died because he was in poor health.

When I told my English teacher, Mrs. Carter, that I was going to move, she took me out into the hall and hugged me tight. She said, "I know you're going to make something out of yourself -- just remember you can be anything you want to be if you work hard at it." I have always remembered those encouraging words.

During the weeks after my father's death, I was angry and blamed my father for putting us in the situation. How did Daddy expect to leave Bessie Lee for Vivian, have three kids with Vivian, and 25 years later bring those three kids back to Bessie Lee, who was unable to have children, and have her raise them? I guess every time Bessie Lee looked at us, she thought about our mother.

I didn't know which direction to go next. My entire family consisted of my sister Linda, who was in a physically abusive marriage in Dallas, and my sister Brenda, who was living in Denver with the father of her young child. Brenda invited me to come to Denver to stay with her until I finished high school in the summer.

In early January, we boarded a Greyhound bus for a 20-hour ride from Marshall, Texas, to Denver, Colorado. I was scared and unsure how Tammy would handle such a long bus ride at her young age. The 20 hours seemed like 20 years, but eventually we reached Denver.

My sister Brenda and her husband Jamel picked us up from the bus station. I explained to them that my social security check would be transferred to their address and, if they would just give me until the end of the semester, I would find my own place. Tammy and I slept on the sofa. But immediate plans were made to move to a much bigger apartment, with a fireplace and swimming pool. I was told exactly how much was needed from my social security check: most of it! I thought Brenda and Jamel were trying to take advantage of me. In hindsight, I know that two families staying in a one-bedroom apartment was not the best arrangement for any of us. The move was necessary, but at the time I didn't understand. When I began to ask questions about the upcoming move, both Brenda and Jamel became furious. I knew then that my next move was just around the corner.

Two months later, Tammy and I moved into a one-room efficiency. All my furniture came from thrift stores and garage sales. I was afraid when it was time for bed, so each night I wedged a chair against the front door.

Once we got settled, I made an appointment with the clinic in my area for a checkup. I decided to begin taking birth control pills. I was determined not to become pregnant again without being married.

I started to go with a young man named Robert who was a year older than I. I was crazy about him. Robert lived in the fast lane. He loved to party, while I was accustomed to staying home with Tammy. We were invited to a party being given by one of his friends. I found a babysitter and went with Robert. We got there and danced a few times. People were mingling and just standing around talking. Robert's friend lit up a joint and started to pass it around. When the joint got to me, I said "No thanks," and passed it to the next person. Several people kept saying, "Just try it." I refused. Everybody said I was a square. I still refused.

About a month later, Robert slapped me during an argument. I was forced to examine my relationship with him. I didn't need a dope-smoking, abusive boyfriend. I made up my mind to end the relationship. Abuse, whether verbal or physical, was not acceptable. Neither was drug use. I'd seen too many of my friends beaten on a regular basis by their boyfriends or husbands.

Robert cried and told me it would never happen again. He begged me to give him another chance. I thought it over and decided not to see him anymore. Tammy needed a stable, healthy environment. I knew that if I took him back, sooner or later he'd hit me again. He kept saying he loved me, but I told him, "You don't hit the people you love." I stopped seeing him and refused to talk with him on the phone. After about two months, he finally gave up.

When I was a child living with Bessie Lee I didn't have control over the abuse, but now I did. There would be no abuse to either Tammy or to me.

Because Brenda worked at night, she had continued to keep Tammy during the day while I went to school. When Brenda and her family decided to move to Midland, Texas, again I was all alone. I was still struggling to graduate from high school in June. With only three months remaining, I was desperate to find a babysitter for Tammy and graduate as scheduled.

Finding a good babysitter for Tammy in Denver was almost impossible because Tammy was a spoiled brat who wanted to be held all day. She was so cute with her big dark eyes and long silky hair. Everyone fell in love with her at first sight -- until they spent an hour with her. It was the same process over and over again. I'd hear about a great babysitter. Once we met, she couldn't wait to keep Tammy. But usually the sitters only lasted a week or two, and two ladies only lasted a day.

The first morning I dropped Tammy off, the babysitter was thrilled. She said she was so happy to be able to stay home and keep kids. Tammy was her first. At the end of the day when I arrived to pick up Tammy, the babysitter informed me that she had decided she didn't want to stay home. She was going back to work. Tammy had cried the entire day.

The second one-day incident happened on a day when I had a test that couldn't be missed or retaken at school. I dropped Tammy off at her new sitter's house. Inside was a huge German Shepherd that looked like it weighed 300 pounds. Tammy became hysterical. The sitter assured me that Tammy would be fine and that the monster didn't bite. I felt so sad leaving Tammy while she was screaming, but the sitter seemed gentle with her. I walked out and shut the door behind me. I didn't want to go to school, but I had to take the test. I stood there for just a second and heard the woman scream "Shut up" at the top of her lungs. I cried all the way to school. I took the test first period, and as soon as it was over I ran in the snow all the way to get my baby. Because I was scared of the dog, I didn't give a reason for picking Tammy up early. I never went back.

The funniest sitter was a lady from Afghanistan who lived in my apartment building. We communicated with our hands and head shaking. By the end of the day someone had taught her a few words of English. When I picked Tammy up at the end of the day, she shook her head and said "No keep."

A friend at school gave me the number of a good babysitter who lived near the school. She kept Tammy the last few months while I managed to graduate.

As I struggled to finish school, many people helped me. One incident in particular confirms my faith and belief in the kindness of all people -- regardless of race or color.

During the early months of January and February, I walked Tammy to the babysitter each day in the snow. I carried her because it took too long for her to walk. I also had to carry my school books and her baby bag. The walk was four blocks. My daily journey began before 7:00 a.m. because I had to be at school by 8:00. One morning a white lady pulled up and rolled down her window. She said, "Honey, I see you in the mornings carrying your baby. I don't know where you're going, but wherever it is, you go every day." I told her I was walking to the babysitter so I could go to school. She said, "My name is Rose, and my husband would kill me if he knew I picked up somebody I don't know, but I just can't let you keep walking with that baby. Come, get in, and I'll give you a ride." It felt so good to ride in a car with the heat on for those few blocks. I rode with that lady until school ended. We didn't exchange numbers, and I never saw Rose again. I will never forget the kindness she extended to us.

When I look back on how many babysitters Tammy had during that three-month period I shudder, thinking of all the new faces and voices she had to adjust to.

I also wonder how I made it. Many days when it was time to get up, I would cry because I was so tired.

Graduation day came, but I was too exhausted to attend the ceremony. My diploma was mailed to me. It holds special meaning because of the adversities and hardships I went through to earn it.

Chapter Six

Working Hard

That summer, I was having trouble stretching my social security checks, especially at the end of each month. I decided to apply for food stamps. I was living on $238 per month of social security benefits. The welfare office was busy, noisy, and nasty. Unkempt women and children were all around. Some of the mothers carried belts or little switches from trees to keep their kids in order, but it wasn't working. The office workers were rude and demeaning. I qualified for six months of food stamps -- $43 per month. When the six months were up, I thought about going back but I didn't like the way I had been treated. I never went back, and that was the extent of my "public assistance."

At the age of 19, when Tammy was three years old, we moved into the Dahlia Apartments in Denver. I met a lady named Vera Taylor who was 13 years older than I. Vera had three children: Marcus, Monica, and Marty. Our kids became fast friends. She was a surrogate mother, confidante, and friend. We spent many hours sitting at her kitchen table talking. When Vera realized I couldn't cook at all, she taught me. I learned to prepare fresh greens and to make sweet potato pie with scratch crust. She taught me to use coupons and spend $20 for groceries that would last a whole week. I bought staples: beans, rice, and fresh vegetables. Our kids played together on the weekends. Vera kept Tammy whenever I needed. She bought me pots and pans, and gave me money from time to time because she knew I was too embarrassed to ask for a loan.

During the summer after graduation, I had two minimum-wage jobs. The worst job was working in the laundry section of a cleaners. I was hired as a temporary stamper. My job was to stamp a number on the clothes with a machine that was heated. On Monday evening, my co-workers started to complain about the nursing home laundry that came in each Tuesday. I had no idea that the reason for their reluctance was the condition of the laundry. The clothes from the nursing home were filled with feces, blood, and stench. I got sick each week and started to quit, but I couldn't. I had bills to pay, and I had to keep my job. Each week, I came up with a new way to combat the smell. My co-workers looked forward to each Tuesday to see what I'd come up with to mask the smell. I wore gloves, pinned a cloth around my nose, and brought air freshener. You name it, I tried it. I worked at the laundry for eight weeks, but when the full-time worker returned, it was time to look for something else.

Jack-in-the-Box was the closest I ever came to slavery. I applied for a job there and followed up each week until finally I just wore the manager down and he agreed to give me a job.

My first day there I was introduced to the assistant manager, Emmitt. He was a young white man who gave orders like a slave driver. I was hired to work the register. But, as soon as he laid eyes on me, I was not allowed to work behind the counter. I spent each day mopping the entire lobby area and cleaning the men and women's bathrooms. As soon as I arrived at work, he would either have a bucket of mop water waiting for me or instruct me to make some. The other workers stood around and visited, laughing at me as I tried to mop around them. Emmitt would hand me a batch of rags and say, "Clean all the silver." The entire cooking area, the countertops, floor strips, and bathrooms were silver. But one night everything changed. As I worked on cleaning all the silver in sight, an argument started in the kitchen. Emmitt had made a worker mad, and she quit on the spot. That left only the two of us. About that time, a large yellow school bus drove up, and off hopped an entire football team and a cheerleader squad. Emmitt was almost hysterical.

He immediately told me to wash my hands and get behind the register. Finally, I'd get to take some orders and work the cash register.

To the first person in line, I said, "May I help you?" Emmitt was at the grill dropping fries, but he immediately appeared and said in his nastiest voice, "Cynthia, in training you learned to say: 'Welcome to Jack-in-the-Box, may I please take your order?' That's the way you say it."

I was embarrassed and angry. All those weeks I had begged to work the counter and wasn't allowed to, but now I had to go by the book. I'd forgotten exactly what the book said. Each time I took an order, Emmitt corrected me in front of the customers or found faults. I finally had enough and said, "I'm doing the best I can, and if that's not good enough I'll just leave." He replied, "You can't leave now, and if you say anything else, I'm going to punch you out." Emmitt was going to punch me off the time clock until I cooled down. So I told him, "Even better than that, I'm punching myself out -- I QUIT!" He said, "You can't quit, we've got all these customers." I said, "Just watch me." A hysterical look came over his face that was almost comical. I wanted to laugh. I punched out and left him there alone. I felt liberated as I walked out and left him to face the hungry, angry group of customers.

The demeaning, low-wage jobs I worked that summer made me eager for school to begin. I realized I had to continue my education.

Chapter Seven

A Skill

I really wanted to go to college, but I had to get a skill so I could get a decent job. I picked up a newspaper and saw an advertisement for Parks School of Business, an executive secretarial school in downtown Denver. Since I enjoyed typing and office work, I called to schedule an appointment. Parks was a reputable school that had a one-year program for an executive secretary certificate. I talked to the counselor and applied. I was accepted on the spot and qualified for a small grant to help with my books and expenses. School started in September from 8:00 a.m. to 4:30 p.m. daily. I had a part-time job at Gunther's Beauty Supply from 5:30 p.m. until 8:30 p.m. Things were falling right into place.

I rode the city bus four times each day. I got up at 5:30 a.m., dressed myself and Tammy, and caught the first bus to the babysitter. After dropping Tammy off, I caught my second bus to school downtown. After school I caught my third bus of the day to collect Tammy. I got back on the fourth bus and rode back near our house. Tammy stayed with my girlfriend until work was over. After work, I walked across the shopping center, picked up Tammy, and went home to do my homework. Exhaustion began to take over, but I refused to give up and quit school.

As school continued, the four bus trips each day began to take a toll. The winter months were especially hard. Morning would come so quickly that I would just hop up and put on the first piece of clothing that I touched. I no longer had the energy to curl my long, black hair, so each day I pulled my hair into a ponytail at the back of my head.

One afternoon, the owner of the beauty supply, Mr. Gunther, told me he wanted to see me in his office. I had only been at work about 20 minutes. A rush of excitement came over me, because I figured he was getting ready to give me a raise. Mr. Gunther was a successful black entrepreneur. I looked up to him. I went upstairs with a big smile on my face. He asked me to have a seat. I was so tired I appreciated being able to sit for a few minutes.

He looked at me and said coldly, "Cynthia, the next time you come to work dressed like this, I'm going to have to let you go." As soon as he got the words out of his mouth, I began to cry in loud, wailing sobs. I cried about not knowing my mother, about my daddy dying, about being tired -- everything. Mr. Gunther didn't know what to say or do. I was so hurt by his words. I kept thinking of how I was trying to do something with my life instead of just giving up. I was in school, working, and taking good care of my child. His comment was the most humiliating experience of my life and remains vivid in my memory, because I can still remember exactly what I was wearing that day. My black pants and gold shirt were both wrinkled. I wonder why he didn't start the conversation by asking if I had a problem. But he didn't. Instead he delivered his stinging insult. I could tell he was embarrassed after witnessing my response. I explained my situation and promised to try and improve my appearance.

For nine months, I worked on improving my appearance and maintained the grueling schedule Monday through Friday. In spite of that humiliating experience, I believe Mr. Gunther reinforced my efforts to succeed. That experience helped me make up my mind never to give up my struggle and to see it through until the end. Mr. Gunther's comments laid the groundwork for me to evaluate myself objectively and accept constructive criticism.

Chapter Eight

A Real Job

I learned valuable office skills at Parks. My typing speed was up to 80 words per minute. Soon I could take shorthand at 120 w.p.m.

Graduation was approaching. Once again, I didn't get to attend the ceremony, this time because my babysitter canceled at the last minute. After graduation, I went into Parks' placement center to look for a job. The Department of Highway Safety had a secretarial position open, and an interview was set. I bought a new blue suit and had my hair fixed. I was immediately offered the position. The job was stable, the pay was better than I had ever earned, and I would have medical benefits. I quickly quit my part-time job.

I was desperate to buy a car. Each pay day I saved a small amount towards my down payment. When I had $600, I went to a car lot. I dreamed of buying a small sports car with fancy wheels and a sun roof. The salesman took me up and down the rows of shiny new cars. He was eager to help me pick out a late model car. When he asked how much I had to put down and I said $600, his face fell. He led me to the back of the lot. A Pinto and Gremlin sat in the corner. He said to stay within my budget, I could pick between the two. I chose the Gremlin. The car salesman seemed disappointed, but I was happy. The car was white with big black stripes. I was so proud of it. The first night, I kept getting up to look out the window to be sure it was still sitting outside.

All my hard work and the low income jobs had finally begun to pay off. After so many years of struggling and counting every penny, I could finally pay my bills and have some money left.

My supervisor at the Department of Highway Safety, Elizabeth Mead, was a beautiful Jewish lady. She embraced me with open arms and treated me with kindness. Although Elizabeth and I seemed to be from different worlds, we each learned about the other's culture. I also worked closely with a lady named Francine who was near retirement age. Our office prepared labels for a monthly newsletter to be sorted by zip code. Francine would mix up the labels, and Elizabeth would ask me to straighten up the mess. Once after I became angry, Elizabeth told me that she wanted to pass on a saying to me that would affect me the rest of my working career. She said, "It all pays the same. Think about it -- whether you are straightening up Francine's mess or starting on a new project, won't your check be the same on payday?" I thought about it for a few minutes and began to nod my head yes. The rest of the day I kept thinking to myself over and over again, "It all pays the same." Since that day, whenever I am asked to do something

55

unpleasant, I think of Elizabeth Mead and her philosophy that "it all pays the same."

My budget was so tight that if something unexpected came up it caused a major setback. Once, my car broke down. After paying the bills and buying groceries, I had $8 left for the two weeks until the next payday. I was determined to make it. Borrowing money from someone was out. I was too embarrassed to ask anyone for help. I fixed our lunches each morning and gave Tammy money for a drink. When work was over, I came straight home, being careful not to use any extra gas. My car didn't move until it was time to go to work again.

The first week ended, and I had only spent about $3. I began the second week and by Tuesday, with three days left, I still had $4. A group of co-workers were going out for ice cream and invited me to go along. I cringed, because I was afraid to spend any money. But I didn't tell them that. I just said I was going to keep working. They refused to go without me, so finally I went along. As we stood in line waiting our turn, I decided to go ahead and get a scoop -- it cost only 75 cents. My mouth began to water for a sugar cone. When my turn finally came, I leaned over and in a whisper asked the clerk, "Does it cost more if I get it in a cone?" She smiled and said, "No -- it costs the same." Ice cream never tasted so good! When payday arrived on Friday, I had exactly 63 cents left.

My budget kept forcing me to improvise. I had to wear dresses to work at the Department of Highway Safety, and just the cost of keeping good stockings on hand started to be a problem. A co-worker gave me a tip that saved money on stockings. If I got a run in one leg and the other leg was good on two separate pairs of stockings, I cut off both bad legs. I was left with a good leg on each pair. I put on the first pair, then the second pair. Now I had expensive "control top" hose because I had on two tops. Even now in a pinch, I'll resort to "clipping" those bad legs to make a good pair.

Around Christmas 1976, I met Frank, a chef who was seven years older than I. Frank was handsome and wore expensive clothes. It was love at first sight. Frank was really a gentleman. He opened the car door when we went out together. He loved to go to the movies, dinner, and dancing. I thought I had finally met Mr. Right, but there was one problem. Frank took me to places that were only for adults. He would call and say, "I have tickets to the movies. Can you find someone to keep Tammy?" When Frank came over to visit he was always nice to Tammy, but I noticed he didn't play with her or plan outings that included her. I thought he just needed time to get to know her better.

After I'd known Frank about four months, he told me he had a special night planned. He told me to really dress up because we had reservations at a fancy restaurant. I was so excited. Friday night came, and Frank arrived with roses. When we got to the restaurant, he pulled a little box out of his pocket. Frank opened the velvet box and took out a beautiful engagement ring with a large diamond. He asked me to marry him. I was so shocked that I didn't know what to say. I hugged him but didn't answer, so he assumed the answer was yes.

In my heart, I knew I couldn't marry him. I believe Frank really loved me, but he just tolerated Tammy. Marrying Frank would have made Tammy's life miserable and lonely. I thought of my daddy's decision to marry Bessie Lee and how it affected me. I couldn't let Tammy suffer the way I did. Once again, I sacrificed for Tammy's happiness. After about two weeks, I returned the ring, and shortly afterwards Frank and I broke up.

Chapter Nine

Close to Daddy

I was content in Denver until Tammy began to ask questions about her dad. "Why doesn't he ever call me?" "Is he mad at me?" "Does my daddy love me?" "When can I see him?" I didn't know how to answer Tammy's questions, because I hadn't heard from Curtis Ray since we had moved to Denver six years earlier.

I placed a call to Curtis Ray's mother in Dallas and asked her to give him my number. About two weeks later the phone rang. Tammy answered it and started to scream, "It's my daddy!" She was so excited. He talked to her a few minutes and asked to speak to me. I felt like spitting into the phone. I was jealous and hurt to see Tammy so excited about one phone call from him, but I tried to understand.

He asked for our address and promised to write soon, but six months passed before we received a letter from him. He wrote he loved us both and wished that we were closer so that he could help take care of Tammy and spend time with her. I made the mistake of reading the letter to her. She asked each day if we could go to Dallas. We never got another letter and only one or two more phone calls.

Holidays were lonely in Denver, since we didn't have any close family there. I began to think it might be better to move closer to my family and Curtis Ray. After a lonely Thanksgiving, I decided we would be living in Dallas by the next year. Both my sisters were encouraging me to move. I took the federal civil service test in Denver and requested to be put on a list for Texas jobs.

Within several months, I received a call from a man named John Hodge, director of personnel services in Dallas. He had a secretarial job opening and called to ask if I was interested in coming to Dallas. I had survived the holidays and wasn't sure if I wanted to move. I established a friendly relationship with Mr. Hodge. During the next year, he called me two or three times offering me a job in Texas. I kept changing my mind. Finally, he told me that he wouldn't keep calling me about the jobs. He said to keep his phone number and, if I ever decided to come to Dallas, he would find a job for me. When I finally moved to Dallas in the summer of 1980, Mr. Hodge remained true to his word. He found a job for me the first day I arrived in town.

I was hired as a temporary for a federal agency. Three months later I accepted a full-time job with another agency. I was secretary to four litigating attorneys. I quickly earned the reputation of being a hard worker. The job was challenging, and the atmosphere was great. I enjoyed the job, but the pay was $150 less each month than the salary I had earned in Denver. My budget began to tighten again.

Chapter Ten

Lies, Lies and More Lies

Initially, Curtis Ray seemed excited about our moving back to Dallas. He visited shortly after we arrived and told me he was married to a lady named Marilyn. He promised to pick Tammy up on the weekends and to give me money for her support. The promise lasted less than a month. He began to call Tammy and promise to pick her up, but never show up. Tammy cried and pouted. I tried to console her, but each time he made a new promise he failed to follow through. I asked him to stop making plans and promises he couldn't keep, but he still lied to her. Tammy cherished each moment she spent with him. I became angry and frustrated each time he lied to her. I needed financial support from Curtis Ray, but Tammy needed his love, attention and a stable relationship.

When Tammy was nine, Curtis Ray bought her a pair of cowboy boots. The boots were brown with a nice heel. She came home excited. The first week she wore the boots every day. Each night she pulled the boots off and kept them by her bed. The next morning she would insist on wearing the boots, regardless of the outfit she chose. I relented. The next week, Tammy wore the boots only on Monday and Friday. I wondered why. When I asked, she said, "My dad bought these, and if I wear them every day I'll wear them out too quick. Momma, I'm trying to save these boots, so I'll only wear them on Mondays and Fridays."

Once Curtis Ray called in the middle of the week and told Tammy that on Saturday he was going to take her to Six Flags. She was so excited. This required a new outfit and hair ribbons. As the big day approached, her excitement was overwhelming. I had to work on Saturday, but that wasn't a problem. Curtis Ray was to pick up Tammy at my sister's at noon. Tammy woke that Saturday at 5:00 a.m. and wanted to get dressed immediately. I refused, but dropped her off at my sister's at 7:30 a.m. By 8:00 a.m. she was fully dressed, waiting on the couch. When I returned from work at 4:00 p.m., she was still sitting on the couch, with her eyes swollen shut from crying. Her dad never came nor called. I went into the bathroom and cried. I didn't know what else to do. Curtis Ray repeatedly lied to Tammy. But each time he promised to pick her up and didn't, I was left to comfort Tammy while she cried.

Tammy's half-sister Tasha, who is 18 months younger than Tammy, was Curtis Ray's favorite. He was married to Tasha's mother Wilma, the woman I had encountered when I first took Tammy to see Curtis Ray when she was a baby. Curtis Ray continually rejected Tammy. She always looked for some way to please him, such as planning several months in advance what she would give him for Father's Day, or spending hours trying to find the perfect birthday card. He never acknowledged Tammy's birthday, and probably never knew the date.

Tammy was particularly hurt one Halloween when she asked Curtis Ray to buy her a costume and he claimed he didn't have the money. A few days later Tasha called to tell Tammy about a mask Curtis Ray bought her that cost over $50. Curtis Ray didn't pay child support and rarely gave me any money at all, but during Christmas he became the Messiah. He would pick Tammy up, take her shopping and spend about $300 on her. She could choose anything she liked, and he would buy it. It angered me because this made my few gifts seem insignificant. I never understood the once-a-year bonanza when I couldn't get him to give her $10 per week for lunch money.

Tammy loved the annual shopping trip. Curtis Ray never realized how hard it was to provide for Tammy all year long and didn't seem to care. His wife Marilyn worked the switchboard at his job, and whenever I called to ask him for money, she answered the phone in the coldest voice I'd ever heard. Most of the time, if she gave him the message, he didn't bother calling me back.

Marilyn, who hated for Tammy to visit, had a son from a previous marriage. He had nice clothes, computers, and electronic games. I never understood why Curtis Ray was so willing to help take care of Marilyn's son but refused to support Tammy. I was sick and tired of begging Curtis Ray to support Tammy. I called the Attorney General's office and found it would file for child support on my behalf. I picked up the papers and returned them in a few days with a $20 fee. The receptionist warned me of a backlog, but she also said that since I knew exactly where Curtis Ray lived and worked, maybe I wouldn't have to wait too long.

Chapter Eleven

Moving on Up

When Tammy was in the second grade, I started dating a guy I met at work named Ronald. Ronald was nice to Tammy. We had a long-term relationship that ended eight years later when Tammy was in the tenth grade.

I continued working the federal job. I was sent to a training class for a new computer. I sat next to a nice lady named Judy Gavin who worked for a large energy company downtown. We ate lunch and talked about our jobs. I told her I really liked my job but I had taken a cut in pay to relocate. Judy said her company was hiring. She asked for my name and number and said she would talk to a friend in personnel. I never expected to hear from her again. But surprisingly, two days later she called and gave me the number of Susan, a recruiter at her company.

I called Susan, but when she tried to set up an interview I refused because I hadn't been working long enough to take time off. Susan offered to interview me in the evening, so I agreed. After the initial interview, Susan called to schedule an interview with a manager named Kay Schultz for a secretarial position in the publications department. Kay, a middle-aged lady, and I immediately hit it off, and a day later Susan called with an offer. The job paid $230 more per month than my current one, and I accepted.

Kay had been in the Army, and she was regimented and strict. Work began at 8:00 a.m., which didn't mean 8:15 a.m. Kay operated the office directly by the procedures manual. All general questions were researched in the manual. My secretarial skills were average, and each time I typed a letter or memo, Kay, who had a degree in English, would make it look like a road map with red marks. But she always took time to explain the corrections and why they were necessary.

One of my biggest problems was confusing homonyms, such as "it's" vs. "its." Kay made a list of the correct use of each homonym. She spent a lot of time helping me improve any areas of weakness. I soon realized that Kay was very concerned about me as a person and her purpose was to help me improve my skills, not to criticize. I began to look forward to her reviews as a learning experience.

In turn, I began to make special effort to exceed her expectations. I arrived at work each morning on time, usually 15 or 20 minutes early. I never took off unless it was absolutely necessary. If I completed an assignment, instead of sitting at my desk waiting for her to give me something else to do, I asked her for more work. Soon, I was finding ways to improve the organization of the office on my own. I made an effort to come to work each day with a smile on my face. I tried my best to have a good attitude. Although there were days I didn't feel like smiling, I made a conscious effort to be pleasant. I answered our phones, going out of my way to be professional and helpful to each caller. I tried to leave my personal problems at home. The exception was if Tammy was sick. On those occasions, I always found Kay to be understanding and supportive.

Kay rewarded my dedication and hard work with substantial salary increases. She was my mentor and a friend. Kay asked me once if there was anything I really wanted for my birthday. She told me to make a list and she would pick one thing. I had three things on the list: to have lunch at Neiman Marcus, to leave early one Friday afternoon, or to purchase a new cookbook. Kay looked the list over and announced that, in honor of my birthday, she was granting all three wishes.

Kay allowed me to attend all the computer training classes available and encouraged me to continue improving my skills. Most of all she demanded excellence, and I responded. My highest salary increase in my entire career came under her tenure. Personnel workers said it was the first time they could ever remember an employee's salary being raised 30% within a year. I owe much of my success to this great lady.

Chapter Twelve

Morals and Discipline

Tammy came home excited after her first day of fifth grade. I asked her to tell me all about her day. She was so excited about her new teacher, Ms. Davis. Soon all she talked about was Ms. Davis. I began to get a little jealous. Who was this lady that Tammy talked about each day? I looked forward to meeting Ms. Davis on parent/teacher night. I arrived early so I could spend some time visiting with Ms. Davis. She welcomed me into the classroom.

I introduced myself and told her how much Tammy liked and respected her. Ms. Davis was a short lady with a great big smile. She told me she loved teaching and she loved all of her kids. I began to see why Tammy was so crazy about Ms. Davis. She did not take her job lightly. Ms Davis was committed to the education and well-being of each child entrusted to her. Her classroom was a safe haven for many children. She replaced Tammy's lost lunch money and even stayed after school if Tammy needed extra help with her homework.

I had many conferences throughout the fifth grade year with Ms. Davis. Of all Tammy's teachers, Ms. Davis was her favorite. Ms. Davis was a hit because she combined love, discipline and learning in a healthy environment. Tammy came home once with great big eyes and said Ms. Davis had a great big ruler. If you acted up in her class, she could sit at her desk and reach your desk with this long, long ruler. Each week Tammy had a new story about Ms. Davis.

The next year Tammy wasn't so fortunate. Her sixth grade English teacher, Ms. Wolff, called the second week of school. She said Tammy was talking in class. I had a rule that if you got in trouble at school, you got in trouble at home.

When Tammy got home, she said that the whole class had been talking and that Ms. Wolff was picking on her. I went to the school for a conference and had a very unpleasant experience. Ms. Wolff was a year away from retiring. She was very negative and critical of the entire class. She didn't say one positive thing about any of the students during the conference. I explained to her that Tammy would not be allowed to disrupt her class. I asked Ms. Wolff to call me anytime she had a problem with Tammy. I left the school dismayed, because I felt that Ms. Wolff was a big part of the problem, but I knew better than to let Tammy know I felt that way. She would have taken advantage of the situation.

When I got home, I explained to Tammy that Ms. Wolff was to be respected. She was an adult and a teacher. Tammy whined that she picked on the kids. I told Tammy she could prove to Ms. Wolff that she wasn't a problem by acting like a young lady in her class. Tammy's rules regarding Ms. Wolff's class were to do each homework and classroom assignment on time. I told her not to talk unless Ms. Wolff said it was okay. It was a rough semester, but I was determined to teach Tammy how to respect authority, even in unfair situations. I never spoke a word to her about my thoughts on Ms. Wolff. She finished the semester with a grade of B, and at our last parent-teacher conference Ms. Wolff complimented her. Tammy learned a valuable lesson in respecting authority.

I began discussing sex in our home when Tammy was in the sixth grade. From time to time, I would bring the subject up. Tammy would always act shy, but I discussed sex anyway. I told Tammy my own experience with sex at an early age and warned her against repeating my mistake. I explained that part of my problem was a lack of information and education. My parents had refused to discuss sex with us. Sometimes Tammy would get uncomfortable, and I often felt uncomfortable too, but we were able to discuss the issues. I knew it was better for

Tammy to learn about sex and its repercussions from me than her peers or at school. Over the years, I told Tammy she didn't have to follow in my footsteps, even though the statistics said she would. I discouraged her from having sex too early or having children unless she was married.

During the sixth grade, the choir planned a trip to Six Flags. Tammy was so excited and counted down each day until the day of the trip finally arrived. I had paid for her ticket in advance. I gave Tammy $20 to spend. The morning of the trip, her dad bought her $30. Tammy felt rich. I took her to the school and watched as she boarded the bus for a day of fun and excitement.

I had to pick Tammy up that night at 10 o'clock. The day went by quickly. I tried to stay awake but finally decided to put on my gown and go to sleep. I set my alarm and got up to collect Tammy.

I arrived at the school and was surprised that the bus had arrived early. Parents were collecting their kids and pulling out, but Tammy was nowhere in sight. I waited and waited. Finally, a teacher came to my car and said, "Ms. Cass, we need you to come inside." I got very nervous and thought maybe Tammy had been hurt on a ride. Once inside, I was led to a room where I found Tammy, the band teacher and the assistant principal, Mr. Marks. He said, "Ms. Cass, we called you in because Tammy, Kerri, and Stacy were detained today at Six Flags for stealing pencils." I wondered why Tammy would steal pencils when she had $50 to spend for the day. She still had $23 when she was caught with the pencils. I looked directly at Tammy and asked her if it was true. She said, "Yes."

I apologized to the assistant principal and the band teacher and assured them that Tammy was not off the hook. On the way home, I explained to Tammy that she had disgraced her school, the choir director, and me. She began to cry. I asked why she had stolen. She said one of the girls who had been caught had shown her some pencils and a ring she had taken. Tammy stole 17 pencils before she was caught. I wanted to wring her neck, but I decided to wait until the next morning so I could calm down.

The next morning I explained to Tammy that she could never place blame on someone else for something she did. I didn't want to hear anything about any other girl. I told Tammy that I had raised her to think for herself, not to allow others to make decisions for her, especially when she knew they were wrong. She was totally responsible for the pencils she stole. Tammy was put on strict punishment for several weeks.

I got on the phone and called the pastor of the church we attended. Tammy was crying and begged me not to call him. I told him the whole story. He said on Sunday after church he wanted to see Tammy in his office. He counseled her and prayed for her. That evening she told me she'd never steal again. I was so thankful she had been caught. The next year when we decided to go to Six Flags she fixed her hair in a weird style and came out in dark glasses because she was afraid somebody would remember the pencil incident. I assured her they wouldn't. This episode began and ended Tammy's brief criminal career.

By the seventh grade, however, Tammy had completely lost her mind. She had gone from a sweet little girl to a back-talking, moody little maniac. This period was a pivotal part of our lives, because I could tell that Tammy wanted to have a power struggle with me. I knew if I lost control of her, I would never regain it. She was also under a great deal of peer pressure at school. Tammy was always on punishment for something. Sometimes I ended up being on punishment too, because to keep her in, I had to cancel any plans I might have. Years earlier I would have spanked Tammy, but now she was 12 years old. Talking, reasoning, and finally punishment seemed to work better, but I always reminded her that she was never too big to get a "whipping" in my house. Unlike my parents, I allowed Tammy to give her opinion as long as she was respectful. I believe in the saying, "Spare the rod and spoil the child." When she asked for something and I said, "No," I also took the time to explain why, reminding her that I had the final word. I continued to be in charge and demanded her respect.

Tammy tried to challenge the authority of her teachers. This was unacceptable behavior that I didn't tolerate. One extremely cold winter day I was at home with the flu. The phone rang, and the assistant principal said I needed to come to the school immediately. I had a 102-degree fever and felt terrible. As I dressed to go to the school, I wondered what in the world had Tammy done. I hurried into the principal's office. Tammy sat there looking angry in a room with her school coach and the principal. The coach said, "Tammy is in the office because she cursed in the cafeteria at lunch."

He explained that by accident a student had smashed Tammy's finger with her chair. Tammy cursed so loudly that the whole cafeteria stopped eating. Coach told Tammy that he was sorry her finger was smashed but cursing was not allowed in school. She was given two options: take one lick or to have her parents called.

Tammy wanted them to call me, because she thought I would refuse to let her take a paddling. I took one look at Tammy and asked the principal, "Where do you want her to bend over?" I announced I was going back home to bed. Tammy looked scared to death when she got home that evening. I told her that I wasn't going to punish her since she took her lick, but that she had to respect authority. She agreed and was glad I didn't give her a lick or two myself that night. A few weeks later I got a call from the coach. He called to thank me for supporting him and said Tammy's attitude had improved dramatically. Coach said, "Just between the two of us, I felt sorry for Tammy getting her finger smashed. But if she had been allowed to get away with swearing in the cafeteria, by next week all the students would have been doing the same thing."

Chapter Thirteen

The Layoff

During my third year of employment with Kay, rumors began to circulate about a major layoff. Kay said our department would probably be safe since our group was small. About a week later when I came to work, Kay was in her office crying. I thought perhaps her dog Mike was sick. Later, when she called me in and told me I was being laid off, I began to cry. She assured me that another position would be found for me in the company. The layoff was August 2, 1984. Kay told me I had until January 1985 to interview and accept another position.

Kay had more than 25 years at the company and knew all the managers and supervisors. She told me when the interview process began that she would tell me after each interview if it was okay to accept the job if it was offered to me. As a single parent, I was more concerned with just getting a job -- any job. I went on three interviews, and after each one I returned to the office excited. Kay would begin to ask me questions and get a really stern look on her face as she began to shake her head. Each time I was disappointed, but I understood that Kay was looking out for my best interest. I respected her opinion.

Finally, a call came from an attorney named Mr. Parish in the legal department. Kay spent about 40 minutes on the phone with him discussing all my "finer points." Later Mr. Parish told me he wondered if anybody could be as good as Kay described. By now it was November, and I only had two months to go. I was prepared to put up a good fight with Kay over this one, but she smiled and said, "This is the one." Later she told me I would have been employed indefinitely until I was offered "acceptable" employment. Looking back on the situation, I felt we were in a relay race for my future, and Kay

had passed the baton to Mr. Parish.

Chapter Fourteen

Teenager

Tammy came home excited, jumping up and down and asking if she could try out for the cheerleader squad. She was in the seventh grade at Memorial Middle School in Garland. I told her I'd think about it. She went to bed talking about it and woke early the next morning begging, until I finally gave in. Her friend Pam was a cheerleader in high school, and Pam promised to come to our house each evening to teach Tammy the steps and routines.

Day after day while I washed the dishes, I could see the girls practicing outside. If Pam took a stance with both arms pointed out straight, Tammy would try to do the same. But, instead of pointing her arms out straight like Pam, Tammy's arms would be very limp and her elbows would be bent.

Soon watching the girls practice became a daily obsession. I began to worry that Tammy would not make the team. She was very uncoordinated, but she could jump as high as a grasshopper. It seemed she could touch the sky. She excelled at her jumps and became a little more confident each day. Meanwhile, I was worried that if she didn't make the team, she would be devastated. I kept reminding Tammy that she could do anything she wanted to do if she worked hard at it. As the tryouts approached, I began to see improvement in Tammy's practice sessions. She even practiced after Pam went home in the evenings.

The day finally came. The tryouts consisted of several cheers before a panel of judges and a popularity vote. After watching all the girls who were trying out practice, I began to worry all over again. I knew how much Tammy wanted to be a cheerleader. She was so confident that she would make the team. I sent up a special prayer and drove her to school. Her uniform was pressed and starched to perfection. Her socks and tennis shoes were white as snow. I asked her if she was ready for the challenge. With a frightened look on her face, she said "Yes." I gave her some final words of encouragement and watched as she walked into the school.

The parents were not allowed to watch the tryouts. I waited an hour with the rest of the mothers. It seemed like eternity until Tammy came out of the gym. She came out with a big smile on her face and said, "Momma, I did my best." I said, "Good -- that's all you can do." We would return to the school at 3:00 that afternoon when the results would be posted on the gym door. We had two hours to go. I also began to plot my strategy for Plan B in case Tammy didn't make it. She had seen a dress in the mall she wanted a few weeks earlier. I knew if she didn't make the team she would need to be cheered up. I had saved money for the dress.

At 2:30 she said, "It's time." It only took us seven minutes to get to the school from our house. We got in the car, and I took the long way to the school. Tammy and I were both nervous wrecks. When we pulled up, the list was already posted. I started to get out, but Tammy asked me to wait in the car while she went up to the door. I was on pins and needles waiting to see her response. She peered at the list on the door and began jumping like a kangaroo, screaming. I got out of the car and started to scream and jump too. She made it! We learned later that Tammy's popularity score with the students had helped her score.

Tammy's focus began to shift away from Curtis Ray to her friends. She was always proud for me to come to school or attend an event because I was the youngest mother among her friends. She always insisted that I "look right." She never allowed me to be dressed out of style because we might run into some of her friends. If we decided to go to the store and I came out in something tacky, she'd just laugh and say, "Where are you going dressed like that?" I'd say, "I thought we were going to the store," and she'd say, "Not with you looking like that -- your pants are too short -- are you expecting high flood water?" Laughing, I'd change my clothes. I learned early on to respect Tammy's opinions and values because her feelings mattered to me.

One of our most embarrassing moments occurred when Tammy was in the seventh grade. I had taken a day off from work. I overslept, but jumped up when Tammy told me she had a test -- we had 15 minutes to get to the school. She hurriedly began to get dressed while I searched for something to throw on. Because I always tried to stress that being on time was important, I was determined to get Tammy to school on time for the test. When she said, "You're going to make me late," I said, "No, I'm not, just give me a second to throw something on."

This happened in the middle of the winter when the weather was very cold. I had on a long flannel gown with a big ruffle at the bottom. I couldn't find any matching socks, so I put on two footies, one green and one orange. Shoes were scattered in the closet, and the first two that I could find alike were beige high heels. I put those on and threw on my coat. I knew I wasn't dressed right, but I thought it was okay to drop Tammy off since I didn't have to get out.

The school had a circular driveway. You could drive in, let your child out and drive back onto the main street. I turned off the car to dig into my purse for Tammy's lunch money. She kissed me goodbye and jumped out, running into the school. I turned the ignition to start the car, but it made a weird sound and wouldn't start. I kept trying, but to no avail. Just as I put my hand on the door to open it, Tammy came running out of the school as if she was on fire. She ran to the car and said, "Momma, please don't get out -- look at your clothes." I said,

"Tammy, the car won't start." She said, "I know, but would you at least wait until the tardy bell rings before you get out of the car?" She looked at me pleading with those big eyes, and I said okay. When the tardy bell rang about three minutes later, I took off my orange and green footies, got out and raised the hood. I went to a nearby phone booth and called my auto club. Thirty minutes later, the repairman showed up. My battery was dead. I learned a valuable lesson that day -- never leave the house without being presentable.

I encouraged Tammy to be active in extracurricular activities. She attended all the dances, parties and skating events held. I dropped off, picked up, and chaperoned as many activities as possible.

Middle school was expensive. Again, I talked to Curtis Ray about paying child support. He laughed in my face.

Chapter Fifteen

Child Support

I had tried years earlier to establish child support through the Attorney General's office by completing an application and paying a $20 fee. I had continuously asked Curtis Ray for support since Tammy was seven. He gave me $10 or $20 every four or five months. He always had a long list of excuses about why he couldn't help, but his lifestyle showed the true measure of his financial status.

By the time Tammy was 15, Curtis Ray was making good money. He was separated from Marilyn and living with his girlfriend. He had a new truck and a Corvette. He spent his time off work playing semi-pro football. I finally got up my nerve to give him an ultimatum. I told him I wanted $10 each week for Tammy's lunch money. I warned him that, if he didn't cooperate this time, I would let the child support office deal with him. He said, "Do what you have to do; I don't care."

Curtis Ray had been threatened so many times he didn't take me seriously. I gave up on the Attorney General's office and contacted an attorney recommended to me by a friend. The attorney's name was Phyllis Gates, and as soon as I heard her voice I liked her. After I explained my situation she said, "First of all we must establish paternity -- but I want to tell you right now, if this is some kind of love spat, let's not go any further. I don't want to waste your money or my time. But if you're really serious about this, I'll get your money."

I set up an appointment for later in the week. Phyllis didn't accept partial payments and told me she needed $1,000 up front to start the case. I had exactly $118 in my savings account. I almost backed out because I kept thinking how the car needed tires and Tammy needed clothes. I knew $1,000 would have paid for most of our immediate needs. But I also knew Tammy was 15, and it was now or never. I went to the credit union and applied for a $1,000 loan. I was still working for Mr. Parish, and I had stable credit. The loan was approved the same day. My hand trembled as I put the check in Phyllis' hand, but it was the best $1,000 I ever spent. She quickly completed the paperwork, and she never left me wondering about the status of the case. Curtis Ray was served with the papers, but he refused to respond. I predicted he would ignore them. Phyllis said no way; he wouldn't be that crazy -- but he was. Our court date arrived. I caught the bus and said a final prayer hoping the judge would order Curtis Ray to pay me at least $100 a month. I was so nervous as I got off the elevator in the courthouse. Phyllis was waiting for me and told me to calm down.

The judge asked me to describe Curtis Ray's lifestyle. As I began to describe his cars and home, the judge became visibly angry. I completed my short testimony. She asked Phyllis a few questions and ruled in my favor. *Five* hundred dollars was going to be garnished from Curtis Ray's paycheck each month. By that time I had weak knees, and I wanted to scream to the top of my lungs. I hugged Phyllis. Instead of riding the bus back to work, I walked, swinging my arms and grinning from ear to ear.

I decided to let Curtis Ray find out about the garnishment from his employer. About two months later I was busy at work when my phone rang. On the other end of the line I heard a hysterical screech that sounded familiar, followed by a barrage of four-letter words. It was Curtis Ray, who had just received his first check minus the garnishment for child support. He cursed, called me names, and continued to scream. I quietly put him on hold and moved into an office and closed the door. I reminded Curtis Ray of all the years that I begged him to help me. I told him he could have saved $460 per month if he'd given me the $10 per week I had asked for. I told him that for 15 years I'd taken care of Tammy, and now it was

time for him to help. I said goodbye and hung up.

Chapter Sixteen

High School

Tammy's first year at Garland High School sailed by. At the end of the year she got a summer job at a Burger King located about a mile from our apartment. Tammy was hired to work a split shift. She began work at 9:00 a.m. and worked until the lunch shift ended at 1:00 p.m. She walked back home. The second part of her shift started at 4:00 p.m., which meant she had to walk back in the heat of the day. That particular summer was one of the hottest summers in history. I picked her up when the shift ended at 8:00 p.m.

Day after day Tammy complained about the walk to and from Burger King. I felt a little sorry for her, but I kept thinking about all the walking I had done and the buses I rode when she was a child. I told Tammy if she quit the job not to expect me to buy her name brand clothes for the upcoming school year. I shared with Tammy my experience years earlier at minimum wage jobs. At least she wasn't mopping and cleaning the toilets! When Tammy got her first paycheck, the complaining stopped. She anticipated each check and bought her own school clothes.

Summer ended, and Tammy asked if she could transfer to the Health Magnet High School because of her interest in the health field. Because Health Magnet was a Dallas school, we moved from Garland to Dallas the summer before she began tenth grade. Part of her curriculum was to have part-time employment in a hospital, and soon she was working an intake desk at a large hospital. She has never been without a job since the Burger King job.

In the tenth grade, Tammy met a boy named Jerome who was a year older than she. I could tell she liked him more than anybody else that called. When the phone rang, Tammy almost broke her neck getting to it. A wide grin came across her face when she heard Jerome's voice.

The day finally came for me to meet Jerome. As soon as I laid eyes on him, my maternal instincts told me he wasn't the right person for Tammy. But I didn't have any justification for my feelings toward Jerome -- only a gut feeling.

Soon his conversations with Tammy turned from friendly to violent arguments. He wanted to know her every move. Over and over, I talked to Tammy about breaking up with Jerome. Tammy would say she was going to break up with him, but after talking to him she changed her mind. Sometimes after talking to him, she would stay in her room and cry. I felt Tammy was searching for a male's love because her father had abandoned her. This was painful to watch, because I was helpless. All I could do was continue to reassure Tammy and tell her that I would always be there for her.

Tammy admitted that both Jerome's parents were alcoholics. At 17, Jerome himself had a drinking problem. I was desperate to break them up, but all my efforts failed. I threatened to take her car, phone, and anything else I could think of, to no avail. My girlfriend Clara told me that she had gone through the same thing with her parents when she was young. Clara advised me to stop criticizing Jerome and to concentrate on reinforcing the good relationship I had with Tammy.

Clara was wise. When I stopped griping and complaining about Jerome, Tammy began to pull away from him. Other guys began to call her on the phone. One day Tammy came to me and told me she appreciated my standing by her while she went through her problems with Jerome. She said she was going to break up with him. I didn't believe her, but true to her word, she called him that evening and broke off the relationship. Tammy said she knew all along Jerome wasn't right for her and she had been listening to me.

Tammy had grown into a giving and loving daughter. One day she called me at work and asked what I was doing. It was during my lunch hour and I said, "Just staying at my desk because I don't have any lunch money." I didn't mean it literally. I just hadn't gone downstairs to cash a check. I guess Tammy thought I was flat broke. We said our goodbyes.

About 30 minutes later, the security guard called from the lobby and said I needed to come down to the lobby to see a visitor. I hung up the phone and wondered who the visitor could be -- I wasn't expecting anyone. I caught the elevator down to the lobby. The door opened, and there stood Tammy. I walked over to her and asked, "What are you doing here?" She said, "I came to bring you some lunch money." She handed me a crisp $20 bill. Tears came to my eyes. She said, "Momma, I remember all those years you took your lunch to work so I could have lunch money. Today, I'm proud I can give you some

lunch money."

Chapter Seventeen

The Opportunity

Working in Mr. Parish's office was an education. He was the smartest man I'd ever met. Once after I re-typed a long document for a project that he had done years earlier, Mr. Parish said he believed two words had been left out of a sentence. I read the sentence. It made perfectly good sense to me, so I figured he was a little kooky. But once I compared it to the original draft, I found two words had indeed been left out. Mr. Parish had a photographic memory. He was a genius, but, even more, Mr. Parish was a kind, patient, man.

Tammy was 16. I had been working in Mr. Parish's office for six years, and Mr. Parish had promoted me to be his legal secretary. Two years later the company reorganized, and the junior attorney for whom I had worked was transferred to another department. Mr. Parish was instructed to hire a paralegal. He came to me and said that he didn't want to recruit from outside the company because he knew I was already doing some of the work. He said I was capable of learning the job, but the position required a two-year degree.

Mr. Parish asked if I was interested in returning to school. I was excited and told him I would. He said, "OK, I'll make a deal with you -- if you are willing to begin doing the work immediately, the company reimbursement plan will pay for your degree; but I can't promote you to the position of a legal assistant or give you a salary increase until the degree is completed." I agreed.

The deal sounded easy, but it proved to be quite challenging. In the fall of 1988, at age 32, I enrolled at El Centro Community College. The first semester I took two classes. I was excited about school. I set aside time each day for my homework. During class, I took notes in shorthand. I also taped each class because if I missed an important point, I could replay the tape.

After each class period I typed my notes and began to study them. For each test I made flash cards. Tammy teased me, but once I began to make straight As, she also started to use flash cards as a study aid. I wanted to do my best. I told Tammy never to do just enough to get by and encouraged her to strive for excellence.

I enrolled each semester, including summers, and rode the bus to El Centro in the sleet, snow, rain, and extreme heat. I made a personal commitment to excel in school.

On May 7, 1992, when I graduated with a 3.9 average, Mr. Parish kept his promise and immediately promoted me to legal assistant, with a substantial salary increase.

Chapter Eighteen

Suicide

Curtis Ray was angry about having to pay the child support, but the only way he could punish me was to hurt Tammy. After his check was garnished, he refused to have any contact with Tammy. She called him time after time, leaving messages at work and home. He wouldn't return her calls. Although he was still married to Marilyn, he was living with his current girlfriend, Rene. Tammy stopped by his sister's house. He was there, but he treated Tammy coldly.

After six months, they began to communicate again. He started going to see her at the school. His shiny red Corvette was impressive. Some of the kids thought he was Tammy's boyfriend until she told them Curtis Ray was her father.

Father's Day was approaching. Tammy called Curtis
Ray to ask if he wanted a pressurized car washing hose. He was
busy and asked Tammy to call him back on Thursday evening.
On Thursday evening, I was in the living room with company
when Tammy told me I had a phone call. Her cousin Sandra
had called and asked to speak to me. I went into the bedroom
and took the phone. Sandra was crying. She said, "My uncle's
dead." I asked, "Which one?" She replied, "Curtis Ray was in an
accident, and he died."

I didn't know how to break the news to Tammy. She
had just talked to Curtis Ray two days earlier to ask what he
wanted for Father's Day. Their relationship had steadily
improved. All I could think of were Tammy's feelings. I didn't
think about Curtis Ray or feel sorry for him -- only Tammy.

I went into the room and said, "Tammy, I have
something to tell you. There's been an accident, and your father
has passed away." A loud scream arose from her throat as she

fell into my arms. Our friends left, and we both cried on our way to Rene's.

When we arrived, we could tell Rene had been packing. She had been crying, so I gently asked what type of accident Curtis Ray had. She seemed surprised and replied, "He wasn't in an accident -- he committed suicide." Tammy and I both stared at her in disbelief.

Rene told us she and Curtis Ray were in the process of breaking up because he was cheating on her. She'd had enough, she said, because this infidelity wasn't the first time. Since Curtis Ray wouldn't leave, Rene was moving out. She had started to take the pictures down and pack small things into boxes when Curtis Ray left for a job-related training program in Cincinnati. When he called and she told him she was leaving, he caught a flight home. The next day he called her at work and told her he was going to kill himself. She rushed home. When she got there, he was in bed reading a magazine. She dismissed the threat as a joke.

But the following day, she was called home by the police because Curtis Ray had made good on his threat. He shot himself in the heart and died instantly. As I tried to console Tammy, I began to wonder if he killed himself because he was having to pay $500 per month in child support. I felt guilty as I tried to figure out Curtis Ray's motive for taking his life. Rene said he killed himself because she was leaving him, although his family said he surely wouldn't have killed himself over a woman. His death was ruled a suicide.

After Curtis Ray's death, I called his wife to ask for information I needed to apply for social security for Tammy. I asked Marilyn if she would consider giving Tammy, who had turned 16, Curtis Ray's small used car. She refused. Marilyn told me that the beneficiary of Curtis Ray's $33,000 insurance policy was his daughter Tasha. As his widow, she would collect his profit sharing fund. I asked her if Tammy was going to receive anything. She replied, "No, unless Tasha is going to give her something." I sat there stunned and angry. Curtis Ray had left Tammy absolutely nothing. I wanted to cry for Tammy. Although he admitted she was his firstborn child, he refused to recognize her as his daughter.

My concern for Tammy reached beyond the fact that he didn't leave her any money. I knew she'd be hurt because, even in planning his insurance, to Curtis Ray, Tammy didn't exist. When I told her she just looked at me and said, "I guess he didn't care anything about me." I tried to comfort her, but the pain in her eyes was evident. I reminded her that money doesn't replace love. Finally I asked Tammy if she wished I had never gone to court for the child support. I told her I felt guilty about his death. She hugged me and told me I had done the right thing and wasn't responsible for his death. I reminded Tammy our love was more important than the money.

By the time she was 23, Tasha had borne three children by different fathers and was incarcerated in the Texas prison system. Her mother is raising the children. During the times Tasha was free and spending money, Tammy never heard from her. Once in prison, Tasha began to write Tammy letters. Tammy has visited Tasha in prison and sent her paper and envelopes.

Tammy began to receive $750 each month in social security benefits. When she became a junior in high school, I decided it was time for her first car. I'd managed to save $5,000 from her social security money. A lady at work was selling a red, three-year-old Ford Tempo. I was excited, because the price was perfect, and I made plans for her to come to our apartment to show Tammy the car. When she arrived, Tammy came down the stairs, took one look at the car and turned and went back into the apartment. I was dumbfounded. Tammy said the car looked like it was for an old lady and she'd rather not have a car if the Tempo was her only choice.

A couple of weeks later, a credit union member had a navy blue, five-year-old Chevrolet Nova for sale. It had tinted windows and sporty silver wheels. It was love at first sight for Tammy. I bought the car and decided to surprise Tammy at school. On the parking lot, I placed a large pink bow on the hood. Tammy came out after school looking for my car, and I waved at her. She kissed and hugged me right in the front of the school. Soon she passed her driver's test and became an independent young woman.

I told Tammy that she was responsible for buying her own gas and insurance. She seemed surprised, but I explained that I couldn't just give her the car. In order for her to appreciate the car, she had to contribute. Although I could have paid the insurance and given Tammy gas money, she would not have taken as much pride in owning the car. It was time for her to learn responsibility. Her part-time job at the hospital didn't pay much, but it was enough to pay her few bills.

Tammy's last year of high school went by quickly. She continued to work at a local hospital as part of the magnet high school program. I was so proud of her accomplishments. Tammy emerged as a proud young woman with an independent spirit.

Graduation was approaching. It was an exciting time for us. I attended a meeting where a few parents complained about the costs of graduating. I sat there with a smile on my face and my checkbook open. Tammy and I were celebrating her graduation, and the sky was the limit. I reflected back on holding her as a tiny baby and thought it seemed like 50 years ago. My baby was graduating.

We had fun shopping for new outfits for the senior activities. Tammy wanted a dark green dress with sequins for the prom. We searched all over town, but couldn't find the right dress. She asked if it could be custom made. I found a seamstress, the pattern, and the sequined material. Dyed shoes and a handbag matched perfectly. Prom night was busy and tense. As Tammy ran all over the apartment getting ready, I sat on the couch with a big smile on my face. Her good friend Dexter took her to the prom. After the prom Tammy came home, changed clothes and went to a senior party. She came home late. We were both exhausted and slept until noon the next day.

The graduation ceremony was held at a large college auditorium. I sat there with tears streaming down my face as Tammy walked across the stage to receive her diploma. Once again, we had beaten the odds.

Chapter Nineteen

Success at Last

I had always dreamed of owning a house. One afternoon I picked up a magazine that advertises real estate in various parts of Dallas. While looking through the magazine, I found two houses in the magazine that were reasonably priced. I figured the location would be run down but took a chance and called the real estate agent, Ron Williams. He was friendly and asked me to drive by and look at both houses and, if I liked either one, to stop by and see him.

The first home was adorable, but it was located close to a large apartment complex. A few blocks away, however, the second house was immaculate. I knew it was *my* house. The lawn was well manicured, and the house appeared neat and well kept. Light and dark pink begonias were planted in the flower boxes. I quickly drove to the real estate office, filled out some preliminary papers and handed over a check for $500 in earnest money to Mr. Williams. He did a preliminary credit check and said my credit looked great.

He made an appointment for us to visit with Mrs. Witt, the seller of the house. Mrs. Witt was gracious as she explained that she was the original owner of the house, built 35 years ago. Mr. Witt had recently died, and she was moving to Florida to be near her children. She seemed anxious to sell the house and offered to throw in all of the appliances for one dollar. I was so excited that I couldn't sleep that night. Another tour was scheduled for Tammy to see the house, and she liked it too. Before work, I'd drive slowly by the house, just praying it would soon be mine.

My apartment rent was increasing to $505. Mr. Williams called to say the loan was approved, and the monthly payment would be $518 -- only $13 more than our apartment. A closing date was set. I paid the closing costs with the remaining money saved from Tammy's social security.

We'd come a long way from our one-room efficiency apartment in Denver. Tammy and I would be the first newcomers to the neighborhood in three decades. The day we moved in, I realized we'd be integrating our immediate area and I worried whether our neighbors would accept us. They were all in their 70s and 80s. My worries were unfounded. One by one each neighbor came over for introductions and welcomed us to the neighborhood. Lillie and Bill are the "mother and father" of our neighborhood. They take a personal interest in each neighbor. Lillie welcomes each newcomer to the neighborhood with a homemade pecan pie. We all look out for each other. A strange car doesn't stand a chance in our neighborhood, because within minutes all the phone lines are lit up. I couldn't ask for better neighbors.

Chapter Twenty

Education - the Key to Success

School had become a way of life for me, and soon I missed the challenge. The first month or two of leisure was great -- I rested, caught up on reading, and watched a little TV. Before long, I became bored. I began to consider returning to school to get a bachelors degree.

LeTourneau University, which was located in the area and geared toward working adults, had just been named one of the top schools in the South by *U. S. News & World Report*. It was, however, expensive -- $8,500 for a two-year program.

I approached Mr. Parish and once again found him to be supportive. LeTourneau's program was structured on the "fast track" system. Every five weeks a new course began. The grading scale was tough -- you had to make 92 to get an A. The company approved my enrollment. For two years, I lived and breathed LeTourneau. Mr. Parish allowed me to incorporate homework into my daily schedule.

Finally, I got to attend my first graduation ceremony. I was so proud and nervous as I heard my name called. "Cynthia Amelia Cass"! I walked across the stage knowing once again I'd beaten the statistics and accomplished a major educational goal. I graduated from LeTourneau University at age 38 with a bachelor of science in business management and a 3.6 GPA.

Tammy worked the summer after graduating from high school and decided to go to a nearby community college. She excelled in her classes while maintaining a full-time job. Unfortunately, our hard work made it impossible for her to receive a grant. We both paid her college tuition each semester so she wouldn't have to repay a large student loan.

Tammy decided that she wanted to be in the social work field. Her counselor said she was a born social worker. During her second year, she worked as a substance abuse counselor. In 1994, Tammy graduated from community college with associate degrees in social work and substance abuse. She immediately began going to a local university to complete her bachelors degree.

I had replaced the Gremlin years earlier with a Datsun 200-SX. I kept each car for seven years. On my way to the grocery store, while I was waiting at a light, an 82-year old driver hit me. My car was totaled, and I was slightly injured. Her insurance company paid me $5,000, and I began to search around various car lots for a car. Once again, I was going to the back of the lot to look for the cheapest car. Tammy told me, "Momma, you've been working hard all your life. I'm paying my own bills now. This time, why don't you buy a car you really want?" I thought about it and decided to get my dream car. I had been working for Mr. Parish for 13 years. I had a stable job, a good income, and excellent credit. I thought about the car my Dad had to give up because he couldn't pay for it. I went to a Cadillac dealership.

I walked up and down the lot until I found a navy blue Cadillac I liked, a program car with low mileage. I filled out the paperwork. The dealer gave me the keys and told me to take the car for a spin. I took the car on the highway for a test drive, and it glided like an airplane. I drove back to the dealership. When I tried to hand the keys to the salesman, he shook his head and said, "You've been approved. It's your car now." My car payment was reasonable. I could afford my dream car! After all the years of working hard and only being able to buy what I could afford, I could finally buy something I wanted.

My 20th class reunion at Jefferson High was approaching. When I started Jefferson High, Tammy was three months old. Now she was 21 years old and a successful college student. Back then, some of the kids weren't allowed to talk to me because I had a baby. I had hardly seen any of my classmates since I left mid-semester during my senior year after my father died. I had mixed emotions about attending, mainly because I'd gained weight. I knew all my classmates couldn't look the same either, so I decided to go.

As the date approached, I bought several new outfits. I drove up to the reunion in my shiny Cadillac. As I stepped out, all eyes were on me. One of my former classmates immediately approached me and said, "Hi, Cynthia. How many kids do you have now?" I was floored. There were so many other questions she could have asked: Where do you live? "Are you married?" None of those questions were on the mind of my former classmate. I guess she assumed that because I had Tammy when I was 16, by now I probably had my own ball club. I answered, "One." She asked doubtfully, "The same one?" I replied, "Yes," and proudly introduced Tammy to her.

I had no reason to be ashamed. Against the odds, I'd survived a teenage pregnancy and was a success.

Epilogue

The Future

On March 5, 1998, I arrived home from work and hit the button to play the messages on my answering machine. A voice said, "Cynthia, this is your mother. Please give me a call." She left a phone number with a California area code.

I froze. I called Tammy and she came running into the room. I replayed the message for Tammy. I looked at her and asked, "Who would play with me like this?" Tammy replied, "Momma, the lady said she was calling from California. You've been looking for her. Maybe this isn't a joke. Call her right now."

I sat down on the bed. I told Tammy that I needed to change my clothes first. She kept saying, "Call her."

I changed my clothes.

I checked the mail.

I brushed my teeth.

Finally, I made the call.

My mother, Evelyn Virginia Terry, answered the phone. She started to cry. After 41 years of not knowing my mother, I heard her voice.

I still don't know the whole story of why we were separated from our mother.

On March 7, 1998, Tammy and I flew to Los Angeles. Brenda lives in Los Angeles and Linda, who lives in Florida, also flew to Los Angeles. We found we had three new siblings. My sister Diane is 38. Brothers Barry and Ronnie are 37 and 34, respectively. We had a reunion and are trying to get to know one another.

Tammy recently got a new job utilizing her counseling skills. She is happy and excited about her future.

I plan to promote my book and speak to teen and single mothers, encouraging them not to give up their dream of success.

Cass' Personal Keys to Success

★   Avoid any type of substance abuse. It's OK to be called square, or a wimp. Drugs and alcohol will guarantee your failure.

★   You won't get something for nothing. Don't wait or depend on anyone for sympathy or help. Learn to depend on yourself. The world doesn't owe you a thing.

★   Don't do anything illegal or surround yourself with peers trying to make "fast money." Fast money is usually illegal money.

★   Acquire skills that allow you to find employment. Go to secretarial school, or attend a computer vocational school. Continue your education by going to college.

★ Focus on a goal, and be pro-active to achieve it. Begin by planning small steps that will ensure that you reach your goal.

★ Attitude is the key to your success. I've learned that few things in life can cause failure the way a bad attitude can.

★ Learn to give negatives and setbacks a low priority in your life. Otherwise, you'll spend your time moaning over what's gone wrong. Concentrate and focus on the positive. Soon the positives will outweigh the negatives.

★ Although welfare or other assistance may be necessary, it should only be temporary. Don't make it a way of life.

★ Concentrate on being your child's parent instead of trying to be a "best friend."

★   Establish   paternity   through   the   legal   system
immediately. Your boyfriend is also responsible for
your child.

Cass' Successful Parenting Tips

1)   Spend time daily talking and interacting with your children. Discuss your day, and allow them to tell you about their day. Be active in school events/projects and the PTA. Go on field trips. Help with homework -- even if you can't draw a missile, you can be there to encourage and offer moral support. As an example, I couldn't help Tammy with algebra, but I sharpened her pencils and fixed her a snack. When it became too difficult, I found her a tutor.

2)   Don't believe everything your children tell you, but allow them to voice their opinion and/or give input in a respectful manner.

3)   Go the extra mile -- it will pay off in the end, and your children won't forget it. Pick up and drop off for parties and games. Have the party or sleep over at your house.

Even though you have to contend with the noise and being eaten out of house and home, you'll know exactly where your children are and what's going on.

4) Meet the parents of the children with whom your sons and daughters interact on a frequent basis. In other words, don't just drop off your teenager at a party without going in to meet the parents. You may be surprised -- the parents could be out of town for the weekend!

5) Although you must set boundaries, have fun with your children and their friends. Soon they will accept you and invite you to chaperone events or field trips. Once again, you will have a first-hand view of what's going on.

6) Be active at school. Cooperate and support the teachers; volunteer for activities and the PTA. Encourage

participation in extracurricular activities, even if it means sacrificing your spare time and money.

7) Don't expect the school to parent your children -- that's your job!

8) Don't allow your children to negotiate punishment or discipline. *You* are the parent.

9) Once you set punishment, you must follow through. Be consistent!

10) Set boundaries and limits for your children. There must be consequences for disobedience. Discipline is a form of love and is necessary to raise responsible children.

11) Apologize when you are wrong. It's okay to say, "I'm sorry." You can't be right 100% of the time. Own up to your faults.

12) Don't ever demean your children by saying, "You're going to be nothing, just like your daddy," or comparing them to other children. Look for the good in your

children. Try to find something positive each day and compliment your children.

13) Don't expect your children to do as you say -- they are going to do what they see you do! Set good examples for them to follow.

14) If you're crazy about a man but you can tell he really doesn't like children -- he just tolerates them -- RUN!!! He's not the man for you and your children. He's probably not a good father to his own children, if he has any.

15) Don't leave your children in the company of men or women you have just met. Get to know people well before you allow them to interact with your children. Your children don't need to meet everybody you meet.

16) Physical or verbal abuse must not be tolerated in your home on any level, whether directed toward your children or you.

17) If you meet a man who has children and he's not supporting any of them, don't have another child with him. He's not going to support a child he has with you either.

18) Be a frequent guest at the school -- sometimes unannounced. Have frequent meetings with the teachers. Don't wait to visit the school until you get a failing slip or there is trouble.

19) If a problem does occur at the school, go there with a positive, non-defensive attitude. Don't assume your children are right or the teacher is wrong until you've heard all the facts. When your children are wrong, admit it.

20) Getting pregnant by a man will not make him stay with you. In some cases it will make him leave.

To order additional copies of *Against All Odds: Success After Teen Pregnancy*, complete the information below.

Ship to: (Please print)
Name_____
Address_____
City, State, Zip_____
Day Phone_____

_____ copies @ $9.95 $_____

Add applicable sales tax $_____

$2.00 for shipping and handling $_____

Total amount enclosed $_____

Make checks payable to Fulton Press and mail to:
                    Fulton Press
                    P. O. Box 151634
                    Dallas, TX 75315/(214) 275-4911

To order additional copies of *Against All Odds: Success After Teen Pregnancy*, complete the information below.

Ship to: (Please print)
Name_____
Address_____
City, State, Zip_____
Day Phone_____

_____ copies @ $9.95 $_____

Add applicable sales tax $_____

$2.00 for shipping and handling $_____

Total amount enclosed $_____

Make checks payable to Fulton Press and mail to:
                    Fulton Press
                    P. O. Box 151634
                    Dallas, TX 75315/(214) 275-4911